THE PROCESSING CHAMBER

Chaos to Organization
40 Day Journal

TEMEILA C. DANIEL

CONCISE
PUBLISHING

THE PROCESSING CHAMBER: *Chaos to Organization 40 Day Journal*

ISBN: 979-8-9872196-0-7

Temeila C. Daniel
www.TemeilaDaniel.com

www.ConcisePublishing.us

This Journal Belongs to:

_____

*"For God is not the author of confusion,
but of peace, as in all churches of the saints."*

1 Corinthians 14:33 KJV

I made this journal to help process all of the thoughts, dreams, ideas, new business ventures, and more that pop into my head on a daily basis. I am a believer, sister, aunt, entrepreneur, and more. I am fearfully and wonderfully made and you are too. "Firing on all cylinders", as they say, could seem and is chaotic sometimes. If we want to, "Tap into Our Next", we have to bring organization to the chaos. Your next can be anything you want to accomplish. I welcome you to *The Processing Chamber: Chaos to Organization.*

In these next 40 Days, I want you to allow yourself to think outside of your current box because it's too small for you. I am a firm believer in being honest with yourself and taking a Self Inventory to see what it is that you have to offer. I encourage you to take the Self Inventory before you begin these 40 days and after you have finished to see how you see yourself, your dreams and your vision.

We have to start somewhere and sometime, so why not here and now?
Let's Go!

Temeila

SELF INVENTORY

Below are some things to make you think about YOU. As you begin to move forward, you will think of things that may not be on the page. Write it ALL down. Don't leave anythng out. No thing is too small. That one detail could be your next stream of income.

How do you feel?

_____

_____

_____

What do you enjoy doing?

_____

_____

_____

What are your strengths?

_____

_____

_____

What do you do on your job or in your business ? *List Everything*

_____

_____

_____

If you could start a business or new stream of income today, what would it be?

_____

_____

_____

What are your weaknesses?

_____

_____

_____

How are your relationships? *Family, friends, marriage & etc.*

_____

_____

_____

What are some areas in your life, you would like to improve?

_____

_____

_____

What are the things you want to accomplish?

_____

_____

_____

How are you finances? Do you have a budget?

_____

_____

_____

What are you going to do different?

_____

_____

_____

Thoughts:

Day 1

📅 **DATE:**

_____

_____

_____

_____

_____

_____

_____

_____

DREAMS:

_____

_____

_____

THE
PROCESSING
CHAMBER

_____

_____

_____

_____

_____

_____

_____

_____

THINGS TO DO:

_____

_____

_____

_____

_____

_____

_____

_____

_____

_____

_____

Day 2

📅 **DATE:**

_____

_____

_____

_____

_____

_____

_____

_____

🤸 **DREAMS:**

_____

_____

_____

THE PROCESSING CHAMBER

_____

_____

_____

_____

_____

_____

_____

_____

_____

⏰ THINGS TO DO:

_____

_____

_____

_____

_____

_____

_____

_____

_____

_____

_____

Day 3

📅 **DATE:**

_____

_____

_____

_____

_____

_____

_____

🤸 **DREAMS:**

_____

_____

_____

THE
PROCESSING
CHAMBER

THINGS TO DO:

_____

_____

_____

_____

_____

_____

_____

_____

_____

_____

_____

Day 4

📅 **DATE:**

_____

_____

_____

_____

_____

_____

_____

_____

🔥 **DREAMS:**

_____

_____

_____

THE
PROCESSING
CHAMBER

THINGS TO DO:

_____

_____

_____

_____

_____

_____

_____

_____

_____

_____

_____

_____

_____

_____

_____

_____

_____

_____

_____

_____

_____

Day 5

📅 **DATE:**

_____

_____

_____

_____

_____

_____

_____

_____

DREAMS:

_____

_____

_____

THE
PROCESSING
CHAMBER

_____

_____

_____

_____

_____

_____

_____

_____

_____

_____

_____

_____

_____

_____

_____

_____

_____

Day 6

 **DATE:**

_____

_____

_____

_____

_____

_____

_____

_____

DREAMS:

_____

_____

_____

THE
PROCESSING
CHAMBER

THINGS TO DO:

_____

_____

_____

_____

_____

_____

_____

_____

_____

_____

_____

Day 7

📅 **DATE:**

_____

_____

_____

_____

_____

_____

_____

_____

🤸 **DREAMS:**

_____

_____

_____

THE
PROCESSING
CHAMBER

THINGS TO DO:

_____

_____

_____

_____

_____

_____

_____

_____

_____

_____

_____

_____

_____

_____

_____

_____

_____

_____

_____

_____

Day 8

 **DATE:**

_____

_____

_____

_____

_____

_____

_____

 **DREAMS:**

_____

_____

_____

THE
PROCESSING
CHAMBER

⏰ THINGS TO DO:

_____

_____

_____

_____

_____

_____

_____

_____

_____

_____

_____

Day 9

📅 **DATE:**

_____

_____

_____

_____

_____

_____

_____

_____

🤸 **DREAMS:**

_____

_____

_____

THE
PROCESSING
CHAMBER

⏰ **THINGS TO DO:**

_____

_____

_____

_____

_____

_____

_____

_____

_____

_____

Day 10

📅 **DATE:**

_____

_____

_____

_____

_____

_____

_____

_____

🤸 **DREAMS:**

_____

_____

_____

THE PROCESSING CHAMBER

_____

_____

_____

_____

_____

_____

_____

_____

_____

THINGS TO DO:

_____

_____

_____

_____

_____

_____

_____

_____

_____

_____

Day 11

_____

_____

_____

_____

_____

_____

_____

_____

🔥 **DREAMS:**

_____

_____

_____

THE
PROCESSING
CHAMBER

_____

_____

_____

_____

_____

_____

_____

_____

_____

THINGS TO DO:

_____

_____

_____

_____

_____

_____

_____

_____

_____

_____

_____

Day 12

_____

_____

_____

_____

_____

_____

_____

_____

DREAMS:

_____

_____

_____

THE
PROCESSING
CHAMBER

_____

_____

_____

_____

_____

_____

_____

_____

THINGS TO DO:

_____

_____

_____

_____

_____

_____

_____

_____

_____

_____

Day 13

📅 **DATE:**

_____

_____

_____

_____

_____

_____

_____

_____

🤸 **DREAMS:**

_____

_____

_____

THE
PROCESSING
CHAMBER

_____

_____

_____

_____

_____

_____

_____

_____

_____

THINGS TO DO:

_____

_____

_____

_____

_____

_____

_____

_____

_____

_____

_____

Day 14

📅 **DATE:**

_____

_____

_____

_____

_____

_____

_____

_____

🏃 **DREAMS:**

_____

_____

_____

THE PROCESSING CHAMBER

⏰ **THINGS TO DO:**

_____

_____

_____

_____

_____

_____

_____

_____

_____

_____

_____

_____

_____

_____

_____

_____

_____

_____

_____

Day 15

📅 **DATE:**

_____

_____

_____

_____

_____

_____

_____

💃 **DREAMS:**

_____

_____

_____

THE PROCESSING CHAMBER

_____

_____

_____

_____

_____

_____

_____

_____

_____

THINGS TO DO:

_____

_____

_____

_____

_____

_____

_____

_____

_____

_____

Day 16

📅 **DATE:**

_____

_____

_____

_____

_____

_____

_____

_____

🏆 **DREAMS:**

_____

_____

_____

THE
PROCESSING
CHAMBER

_____

_____

_____

_____

_____

_____

_____

_____

THINGS TO DO:

_____

_____

_____

_____

_____

_____

_____

_____

_____

_____

_____

Day 17

📅 **DATE:**

_____

_____

_____

_____

_____

_____

_____

DREAMS:

_____

_____

_____

THE
PROCESSING
CHAMBER

THINGS TO DO:

_____

_____

_____

_____

_____

_____

_____

_____

_____

_____

_____

_____

_____

_____

_____

_____

_____

_____

_____

Day 18

📅 **DATE:**

_____

_____

_____

_____

_____

_____

_____

_____

DREAMS:

_____

_____

_____

THE
PROCESSING
CHAMBER

THINGS TO DO:

_____

_____

_____

_____

_____

_____

_____

_____

_____

_____

_____

_____

_____

_____

_____

_____

_____

_____

_____

Day 19

📅 **DATE:**

_____

_____

_____

_____

_____

_____

_____

_____

🤸 **DREAMS:**

_____

_____

_____

THE PROCESSING CHAMBER

_____

_____

_____

_____

_____

_____

_____

_____

_____

THINGS TO DO:

_____

_____

_____

_____

_____

_____

_____

_____

_____

_____

_____

Day 20

_____

_____

_____

_____

_____

_____

_____

_____

DREAMS:

_____

_____

_____

THE
PROCESSING
CHAMBER

THINGS TO DO:

_____

_____

_____

_____

_____

_____

_____

_____

_____

_____

_____

Day 21

📅 **DATE:**

_____

_____

_____

_____

_____

_____

_____

_____

💃 **DREAMS:**

_____

_____

_____

THE
PROCESSING
CHAMBER

THINGS TO DO:

_____

_____

_____

_____

_____

_____

_____

_____

_____

_____

_____

_____

_____

_____

_____

_____

_____

_____

_____

_____

_____

_____

Day 22

📅 **DATE:**

_____

_____

_____

_____

_____

_____

_____

DREAMS:

_____

_____

_____

THE
PROCESSING
CHAMBER

THINGS TO DO:

_____

_____

_____

_____

_____

_____

_____

_____

_____

_____

Day 23

📅 **DATE:**

🤸 **DREAMS:**

THE
PROCESSING
CHAMBER

_____

_____

_____

_____

_____

_____

_____

_____

_____

_____

THINGS TO DO:

_____

_____

_____

_____

_____

_____

_____

_____

_____

_____

_____

Day 24

📅 **DATE:**

_____

_____

_____

_____

_____

_____

_____

_____

🤸 **DREAMS:**

_____

_____

_____

THE
PROCESSING
CHAMBER

THINGS TO DO:

_____

_____

_____

_____

_____

_____

_____

_____

_____

_____

_____

_____

_____

_____

_____

_____

_____

_____

_____

Day 25

_____

_____

_____

_____

_____

_____

_____

_____

🎯 **DREAMS:**

_____

_____

_____

THE
PROCESSING
CHAMBER

THINGS TO DO:

_____

_____

_____

_____

_____

_____

_____

_____

_____

_____

_____

_____

_____

_____

_____

_____

_____

_____

Day 26

📅 **DATE:**

_____

_____

_____

_____

_____

_____

_____

_____

🔥 **DREAMS:**

_____

_____

_____

_____

THE
PROCESSING
CHAMBER

⏰ **THINGS TO DO:**

_____

_____

_____

_____

_____

_____

_____

_____

_____

_____

_____

_____

_____

_____

_____

_____

_____

_____

_____

Day 27

📅 **DATE:**

_____

_____

_____

_____

_____

_____

_____

_____

🔥 **DREAMS:**

_____

_____

_____

THE
PROCESSING
CHAMBER

_____

_____

_____

_____

_____

_____

_____

_____

THINGS TO DO:

_____

_____

_____

_____

_____

_____

_____

_____

_____

_____

Day 28

📅 **DATE:**

_____

_____

_____

_____

_____

_____

_____

_____

🤸 **DREAMS:**

_____

_____

_____

THE
PROCESSING
CHAMBER

THINGS TO DO:

_____

_____

_____

_____

_____

_____

_____

_____

_____

_____

Day 29

📅 **DATE:**

_____

_____

_____

_____

_____

_____

_____

_____

🔥 **DREAMS:**

_____

_____

_____

THE PROCESSING CHAMBER

THINGS TO DO:

_____

_____

_____

_____

_____

_____

_____

_____

_____

_____

_____

_____

_____

_____

_____

_____

_____

_____

_____

Day 30

📅 **DATE:**

_____
_____
_____
_____
_____
_____
_____
_____

🏃 **DREAMS:**

_____
_____
_____

THE
PROCESSING
CHAMBER

THINGS TO DO:

_____

_____

_____

_____

_____

_____

_____

_____

_____

_____

_____

_____

_____

_____

_____

_____

_____

_____

_____

Day 31

📅 **DATE:**

_____

_____

_____

_____

_____

_____

_____

_____

🤸 **DREAMS:**

_____

_____

_____

THE PROCESSING CHAMBER

_____

_____

_____

_____

_____

_____

_____

THINGS TO DO:

_____

_____

_____

_____

_____

_____

_____

_____

_____

_____

_____

Day 32

📅 **DATE:**

_____

_____

_____

_____

_____

_____

_____

🔥 **DREAMS:**

_____

_____

_____

THE
PROCESSING
CHAMBER

_____

_____

_____

_____

_____

_____

_____

_____

_____

THINGS TO DO:

_____

_____

_____

_____

_____

_____

_____

_____

_____

_____

_____

Day 33

📅 **DATE:**

_____

_____

_____

_____

_____

_____

_____

🔥 **DREAMS:**

_____

_____

_____

THE
PROCESSING
CHAMBER

THINGS TO DO:

_____

_____

_____

_____

_____

_____

_____

_____

_____

_____

_____

_____

_____

_____

_____

_____

_____

_____

_____

_____

Day 34

_____

_____

_____

_____

_____

_____

_____

🤸 **DREAMS:**

_____

_____

_____

THE
PROCESSING
CHAMBER

_____

_____

_____

_____

_____

_____

_____

_____

_____

_____

THINGS TO DO:

_____

_____

_____

_____

_____

_____

_____

_____

_____

_____

_____

Day 35

📅 **DATE:**

_____
_____
_____
_____
_____
_____
_____

🤸 **DREAMS:**

_____
_____
_____

THE
PROCESSING
CHAMBER

THINGS TO DO:

_____

_____

_____

_____

_____

_____

_____

_____

_____

_____

_____

_____

What's Your Next?

Day 36

📅 **DATE:**

_____

_____

_____

_____

_____

_____

_____

_____

🏆 **DREAMS:**

_____

_____

_____

THE
PROCESSING
CHAMBER

THINGS TO DO:

_____

_____

_____

_____

_____

_____

_____

_____

_____

_____

_____

_____

_____

_____

_____

_____

_____

_____

_____

_____

Day 37

_____

_____

_____

_____

_____

_____

_____

_____

DREAMS:

_____

_____

_____

THE
PROCESSING
CHAMBER

_____

_____

_____

_____

_____

_____

_____

_____

_____

_____

_____

_____

_____

_____

_____

_____

_____

_____

_____

_____

What's Your Next?

Day 38

📅 **DATE:**

_____

_____

_____

_____

_____

_____

_____

🔥 **DREAMS:**

_____

_____

_____

THE
PROCESSING
CHAMBER

⏰ **THINGS TO DO:**

_____

_____

_____

_____

_____

_____

_____

_____

_____

_____

_____

_____

_____

_____

_____

_____

_____

Day 39

_____

_____

_____

_____

_____

_____

_____

🔥 **DREAMS:**

_____

_____

_____

THE
PROCESSING
CHAMBER

_____

_____

_____

_____

_____

_____

_____

_____

_____

THINGS TO DO:

_____

_____

_____

_____

_____

_____

_____

_____

_____

_____

Day 40

📅 **DATE:**

_____

_____

_____

_____

_____

_____

_____

🔥 **DREAMS:**

_____

_____

_____

THE
PROCESSING
CHAMBER

_____

_____

_____

_____

_____

_____

_____

_____

_____

_____

_____

_____

_____

_____

_____

_____

_____

_____

_____

What's Your Next?

SELF INVENTORY

Below are some things to make you think about YOU. As you begin to move forward, you will think of things that may not be on the page. Write it ALL down. Don't leave anythng out. No thing is too small. That one detail could be your next stream of income.

How do you feel?

_____

_____

_____

What do you enjoy doing?

_____

_____

_____

What are your strengths?

_____

_____

_____

What do you do on your job or in your business ? *List Everything*

_____

_____

_____

If you could start a business or new stream of income today, what would it be?

_____

_____

_____

What are your weaknesses?

_____

_____

_____

How are your relationships? *Family, friends, marriage & etc.*

_____

_____

_____

What are some areas in your life, you would like to improve?

_____

_____

_____

What are the things you want to accomplish?

_____

_____

_____

How are you finances? Do you have a budget?

_____

_____

_____

What are you going to do different?

_____

_____

_____

Thoughts:

SELF PUBLISHING MADE
EASY

Let Us Be Your

ONE STOP
SHOP

Ghost Writing
Editing
eBook Creation

Formatting
Cover Design
Distribution

& More

Email Us @ info@ConcisePublishing.us

THE KING and His GLORY (PART 2)
...RE GOLD FROM THE BOOK OF ISAIAH
...BOUT THE COMING KING OF GLORY

GREG HARRIS

Never stop Dreaming

IT WILL WORK THIS TIME

Cecil E. Bridgeforth

LET GO OF THE COOKIES
Do You See What They See In You?

James Edwards

THE LIE
and other
BIBLICAL TRUTHS
from the COMING TRIBULATION

Greg Harris

DELIVERANCE FOR REAL

Dr. Shirley R. Brown, Th.D

WORKBOOK

TEMEILA C. DANIEL

A Guide to Virtual Meeting
NETIQUETTE

GEORGE BLOOMER SCHOOL OF MINISTRY PRESENTS
Warfarecology

ALTARS & UNGODLY COVENANTS

...ISHOP GEORGE BLOOMER

YOU GOT
THE MIDA$

TOUCH
Author of Second in Command

OVERSEER RONNIE KING, SR.

Miss Carter's HANDWRITING

PRACTICE YOUR
ABC's
AND
COLORING BOOK

DOLLETTE CARTER